Male Midlife Crisis

Why It Causes Men To Destroy Their Families, Finances and Even Commit Suicide…and What You Should Do

by Kara Oh

Published by Avambre Press
2375 Foothill Road
Santa Barbara, CA 93105

Copyright© 2014 by Kara Oh

ISBN-13: 978-1505882698
ISBN-10: 1505882699

Table of Contents

Introduction

This book is about male midlife crisis. Yes, it is real and yes, it is the topic of many a joke. But it is a serious subject that needs to be let out into the light of day. Men commit suicide over it; destroy their marriages, their families, their finances, their careers, and their credibility because of it. Who among us hasn't made fun of the guy who goes out and buys a sports car, then dumps his wife for a twenty-something airhead. To most of us, he looks like a complete fool. But to him, it is his attempt to save himself. You'll learn why as you read this book.

Obviously, many men don't 'act out' when they go through those midlife years. I'll explain why that is so you can look at your husband and ascertain whether he is likely to have difficulty in his transition.

Armed with what you will be learning in this book, you may be able to avoid the disasters that other women have had to endure.

Male midlife crisis is a topic that I began studying in 1995. It was a personal quest to determine what was going on with my husband. I'm sure of the date because I just looked at my divorce papers to check. I was divorced after 29 years of marriage in October, 1996. The year before that was horrible and gut wrenching.

For the first 27 years of my marriage, my husband was someone I could count on, someone I knew, and someone I respected. Then he began to change. Before the change, we had always been a team. We had our own careers and interests, but we made decisions together, we were best friends, and we did everything as a couple. In our community, we were a model of the perfect marriage. A single woman, when verifying the gossip she had heard about our impending divorce, broke down and cried, sputtering through her tears, "If you two can't make it, there's no hope for the rest of us."

There was a pivotal moment that began the spiraling down of our marriage. A massage therapist suggested he might learn a lot about himself if he had an affair. He told me what she had suggested and we had a good laugh. But the idea stuck and began to take shape in his mind. After a time, he said he was attracted to a woman he had met and needed to 'explore' what it was all about.

I tried to be okay with what he wanted, but every cell in my body was screaming in outrage. To avoid the gory details, I'll just say that after about eighteen months of struggle and lots of tears, I finally filed for divorce.

From the little bit I was able to find on the subject, my ex-husband was exhibiting all the classic signs of male midlife crisis. I asked him if that was what was going on. He denied it and was actually quite offended that I would suggest such a thing. He insisted that what he was wanted to explore and expand his spiritual side, and his ability to love me more completely.

I continued to insist that loving another was NOT the way to learn to love me more deeply. Today, now that I understand more fully what male midlife crisis is all about, I understand why he was offended by the accusation that he might be going through a midlife crisis.

I'm sure that even today he would deny it, but I'm certain that's what was going on. I tried to understand it. I searched for books on the topic but could not find any help. I had no way of knowing what to do.

I've since learned that it is never okay to tell a man he's going through midlife crisis, or even hint that maybe that might be what is going on. Part of the reason is that society makes fun of it. So what man would admit that he's 'just being foolish.' To them, when they're in the midst of it, it's a very scary, painful time.

There was no way I could save my marriage other than to accept him being with other women. If I'd known what I know today, I might have been able to get through it. But I chose divorce because I could no longer trust or respect my husband. I realized that without trust or respect, there is no basis for love.

Once I was single, I continued my study of men. I was teaching a seminar called *Embracing Our Sensual Selves*. In the afternoon of the last day of each seminar, I invited a panel of men to answer any questions the women had ever wanted to ask a man, no matter how personal. The seminars were a grand success.

To determine if the men on the panels were capable of being open, honest, able to express themselves, and as I often joke, to see if they were 'up' for the job, I interviewed them individually. It was a very enlightening experience for them as well as for me. They told me things about themselves–and men in general–that I had never heard or read. I knew my women friends and the women in my seminars didn't know those things either, because we were all complaining and frustrated about the same things.

So I took what I had learned and wrote my first book about men titled, *Men Made Easy*. In it, I share 12 secrets that every woman needs to know about men if they want to have more satisfying and fulfilling relationships.

Women often shared the frustration they experienced when their husbands or boyfriends were trying to make it through their midlife crisis years. They didn't necessarily know that was what was happening, but I knew the signs when I heard what they described. Having learned a lot more about the subject since that crazy time in my marriage, I decided it was time to write a book on the subject so I could help on a larger scale.

I hope to offer you information that was not available to me when I was going through it. When you understand what midlife crisis is and learn what you can do to help your husband or boyfriend, maybe, if and when he starts going through it, he won't have such a difficult time.

Most important, I want you to be able to help yourself because it can be the most traumatic thing that your marriage will ever have to endure. You must learn what you can do to insulate yourself from his actions as well as keep your sanity. And maybe you will be able to get him to read it as well. But don't count on it.

If he hasn't gone through it yet, maybe you can help him before that frightful time hits. And maybe you can help your sons avoid the booby-trap that society has already set for them.

My blessings to you if you are in the middle of his midlife crisis, and my heartfelt encouragement if your man isn't quite there yet. With what you are about to learn, you just might make it through without both of your lives crumbling around you. At the very least, you won't think he's going crazy, and you will know to stay out of his way if he does not respond to your newfound wisdom.

6

Chapter 1

Male Midlife Crisis: Is It Real?

Is male midlife crisis real? It depends on whether you ask a man who is going through it or a woman who helplessly watches him change into someone she doesn't know.

Few men admit that it is real, even when their lives are crumbling around them. The irony is that the very reason men won't admit they are struggling with a midlife crisis is the same reason it occurs. They are supposed to be what they've been taught to be: men. That means have it all together, have all the answers, do not, *DO NOT*, show any kind of vulnerability, least of all, to feel emotions. Midlife crisis is the antithesis of those social directives.

Your husband, boyfriend, brother, father, and even your sons (whether you like it or not) have been taught to fit into a certain mold which happens to be a very tight fit. So tight that a great deal of what he "could be" has to be discarded or hidden away. All of who he is, or might be, will not fit into that box.

Here are some of the things that don't fit:

- The ability to be vulnerable,
- To make mistakes,
- To do silly things for no reason,
- To express what's in his heart and soul,
- To follow a dream that his family, teachers and peers might think is silly,
- To express his creativity,
- To express his full range of emotions.

All of these are perceived as being weak or feminine, which is, sadly, to them, the same thing.

To survive in this narrow world, he has learned to shut off his feelings and is a stranger to most of his emotions. As you learn more about this potentially life-threatening subject, you'll understand how truly significant the inability to feel is to the dilemma with which most men must struggle. The struggle is life-long, and the crisis explodes when the struggle becomes unbearable.

We joke about, and make fun of midlife crisis because men often do things that appear to be stupid or childish when they are going through it: the motorcycle, the sports car, the bimbo, the new hairpiece, the new body. What man wants to admit to being a joke? So they suffer in silence and often their lives get destroyed with divorce, financial ruin, and even suicide, with no one knowing quite what happened, even the man going through it.

Yes, male midlife crisis is very real and much more serious than most of us can know. Once you understand what it is all about, you will see how terribly insensitive all the jokes and teasing are. It is probably the most serious and potentially devastating thing that men have to endure. The problem is that no one understands it, least of all the man who is going through it. And there is no preparation for its coming. All he knows is that he's dissatisfied with his life; feeling lost, alone, doesn't know why, and doesn't know what to do about it.

Women often write to me and ask if their husband or boyfriend is going through a midlife crisis. They list all the reasons they think that might be what is going on. Intuitively they know that something serious and frightening is occurring, but because they weren't taught how to deal with it, they feel lost, shut out, and frustrated. They want to help if they can, but there is little that they can do.

Because men suffer in silence, (even if they knew what was going on they wouldn't dare talk about it,) no one knows much about it. And certainly, there are no clear guidelines for how to make it through to the other end. You will understand why this is such a tragedy as you read further.

The man who has someone who gives him support and understands is more likely to get through it with less long-term damage. At the other end of his journey lies the possibility that he will become a happier, more sensitive, more fulfilled man. And you will have a closer approximation to the man you always knew he could be.

But that's a big if. Hopefully, after you know what male midlife crisis is, how to negotiate through it, and how to reassemble the pieces he has strewn about him, you will both be more satisfied with your lives.

Chapter 2

The Signs of Midlife Crisis

There are a variety of signs that a man is going through his midlife crisis. Of course, they very with each man as does the intensity of each behavior. But the following list should help you begin to understand what this very serious time in his life is all about:

- His personality changes.
- He gets angry for no reason.
- He loses interest in his work or changes jobs on a whim.
- He ignores his responsibilities.
- He becomes obsessed with his appearance.
- He reverts to boyhood behavior.
- He makes friends with other irresponsible men.
- He spends more time away from home.

- He drinks more or starts using drugs.
- He begins to gamble...a lot.
- You see lust in his eyes when he looks at other women, or worse, you suspect he's having an affair.
- He starts making plans to sail around the world, even when he's never sailed a boat in his life.
- He comes home with a sports car.
- He wants to move out...but he's not sure.
- He ignores his kids, the house, his family, you.
- He's insensitive to how he's hurting the people around him and gets defensive if you even hint that there's something wrong.

Does any of this sound familiar? It does if your man is between 40 and 55 and has been living the typical, 'expected' role of a man. Remember the box he has been forced to cram himself into? He's never acknowledged his 'inner' self, his feeling self, the part that looks inside and questions who he is.

Therapy? No way. He says that's for women and wimps. That would show weakness and that isn't okay. And it definitely does *not* fit into that box of what it means to be a man.

When you start accusing him of changing, of being childish, of wrecking the finances, the family, and the marriage, he strikes out at you, his wife. You begin to fight all the time; he accuses you of things you haven't done and gets angry with little provocation.

And what do you do? You get hurt, frustrated, try to understand, plead for him to get help, maybe even change your behavior patterns in an unsuccessful attempt to placate him. You're walking on eggs all the time, and you're worn out. But nothing works and you watch helplessly as your marriage falls apart.

You try to talk to him about what's going on, but he says nothing is wrong and to leave him alone. You try leaving him alone, but that doesn't work either. Everything in your life is turned upside down and there doesn't seem to be any rational way to deal with him.

"He's always been so even, unemotional," you tell your friends. "He's been my rock, always taking care of us. Why has he turned on us?"

But he isn't turning on you. It isn't about you, at least not directly. It's about that too-small box that he stuffed himself into when he was a boy. He was barraged with messages that taught him how to be a man: "Big boys don't cry. " "Pick yourself up, dust yourself, off, get back out there, be a man." "Fight your own fights, don't be a sissy." "Don't let them see that you're scared."

When they grow up they're told they need to 'settle down,' be responsible, don't feel, don't cry. They're supposed to take care of everyone else, be brave, don't show fear or weakness, and be the strong one.

A man can't even be silly without everyone assuming he's been drinking. Men have to work, marry, take care of a family, and be a model citizen. And never, ever admit that they're hurting, scared, and confused.

The signs may be obvious to you, but to him, they're invisible because he can't, and won't look at what is going on. It's too scary because it is too far out of his consciousness to acknowledge, yet alone accept. And it's too uncomfortable to allow himself to look at what might be going on.

He doesn't understand, and fears he may be going crazy. That's why so many men turn to alcohol, drugs, and sex. And sadly, it's why suicide is most prevalent during these precarious years, other than the teenage years.

He masks and numbs the fear and the ever-present desire to scream, "What's happening to me?" He suffers alone and doesn't know what to do. If he knew to expect it, like women know to expect menopause, he might be better able to handle it.

Not that long ago, no one talked about menopause. Women were committed to insane asylums, calling the problem a mental breakdown. Doctors told women they were imagining their symptoms. Women didn't talk about it so when it hit, so they were as unprepared as the men of today who are suffering through the 'unknown' of midlife crisis.

Today women have shelves of books, lectures, talk shows, and girlfriend conversations that discuss openly all the physical, emotional and behavioral changes that are part of the 'change of life.' Because menopause is now understood, it's no longer feared. And women do not need to suffer in silence, alone, fearing they are losing their minds.

Someday, hopefully soon, there will be as much information available and openly talked about on the subject of male midlife crisis. But until then, you must wade through it as best you can, armed with this beginning of understanding, and maybe, maybe you can help ease the way for yourself and him.

Certainly you can light the path for your sons so they will be better prepared and maybe even less at risk than if they didn't have you there, guiding them. And if you can prepare your daughters, maybe they will be able to walk through it with their husbands. Change takes time, but it all starts at the beginning. This is the beginning, and you are part of it.

16

Chapter 3

What Causes Male Midlife Crisis?

Because boys have been programmed to grow up to be strong, unemotional men, they begin a path toward midlife crisis when they are babies. Studies in hospitals showed that newborn baby boys were held less, allowed to cry longer, handled rougher, and spoken to less gently than baby girls. Their programming begins at infancy, and never, ever lets up.

Little boys are taught not to cry, "Be mama's little man," "Don't be a sissy," "It's only a scratch," "You've got to be tough." They learn from their peers that the worst thing they can be called is "Sissy." In a documentary on young boys, one twelve-year-old boy said he sometimes wanted to cry when he got hurt, but wouldn't dare because the other boys would tease him.

I watched my seven-year-old grandson go through the contortions of not letting himself cry when he was disappointed and embarrassed that he was too short to get on the 'cool' rides at the carnival.

In sports, boys are taught to focus on winning, being tough, taking their falls like a man. Men are taught to focus on achieving goals and being the solid rock in their community and family. And to always ignore the pain. They ignore their health issues until there is no choice, and they're forced to go to a doctor or the hospital. In every area of his life, he hides or ignores what's going on inside.

The programming, the directive to 'fit into that cramped box,' is insidious, because he's taught not to acknowledge or admit that he has all those feelings churning around inside of him. That's part of why teenage boys are the most likely to commit suicide. They are in between being boys and men, with no understanding that they can talk to someone.

So where can a man go to talk about being unsure or scared? Where can he go when he needs to get away from the pressures of being a man? Who can he talk to when he is failing at his job, has lost financial ground, or made a huge blunder at work? You may say you want him to go to you. But he knows you need to see him as your rock, the one who shields and saves everyone else.

If he lets down completely, maybe breaks down and sobs like a baby, would you know what to do?

Would you still be able to look up to him? Would your relationship be the same if you knew how scared he is sometimes? How unsure of himself? If you're honest with yourself, you will have to admit it might make a difference.

I remember in one men's group I was leading, a man shared that he finally felt 'safe' enough to be totally vulnerable with his girlfriend. He shared his fears and frustrations and even cried. He said she changed after that and soon, broke up with him. As he exclaimed to the group, "I'm never doing that again...ever."

Because the life men are expected to act out is so narrow, there often comes a moment in time between 40 and 55 when each man looks back and asks himself, "Is this all there is? Is this what I've been busting my butt for all these years?"

He feels that his life is empty, that something is missing, but he doesn't know what it is. He has no idea that what is missing are all the aspects of his humanness that were ignored when he entered the world, and a blue blanket was placed around his tiny body.

This may be the first time he has ever taken a serious look at his life. It's the time a man finally 'pauses' long enough from being 'the man' to see that maybe there could have been, should have been, more.

The title of this book was going to be *Men - Oh! - Pause*. But an even more appropriately title might have been: *Men - Oh #&*@!!! - Pause* because that is what he often feels when he opens his eyes and looks clearly at the life he was directed to live. When he takes that moment to pause and question, he often finds himself in a free-fall with not bottom in sight and "Oh #&*@!!!" is all he can feel.

The questioning is usually unconscious, just a feeling in his gut. He is completely unaware that what he is experiencing is doubt. Doubt in his abilities as a man, doubt in his abilities to take care of his responsibilities and obligations, doubt about the choices he made.

Sadly, many of his 'choices' were made by others; his father, mother, teachers, coaches, society. Sometimes he chooses a particular job simply because he needs to make money to support a wife and growing family. Now, after living a life that was very likely not his deepest heart's desire, he feels the emptiness, and all he knows is that he's not happy. There is a sense of loss. So he mourns, but for what he is unclear.

What about men who, from the outside, look like they 'have it made,' are living the dream, and envied by others? They feel the same doubts and fears as men who have fallen very short of what they thought their life was going to be.

The more unconscious a man is about what is happening to him, the more likely he is to act out in ways that appear foolish. He might dump his wife for a younger women, get the sports car, a Harley, a new wardrobe, new hair-do, start working out like a demon, getting spray tanned, or even changing to a new job.

Or maybe he goes in another direction and starts to drink more, take drugs, hang out in places he would never have been seen in before the crisis began. Maybe he just does more of the same and works harder and longer hours. Anything to keep from feeling the pain that is erupting through every pore of his body.

Or sadly, he becomes a statistic and takes his life because he can't deal with the inner questioning, the doubts, and the disappointment that is staring back at him in the mirror. More men than women kill themselves and the older they get, the higher the numbers go.

Even if a man could identify what was going on, he would not know how to talk about it. And most men feel they have no one they can talk to. If they do attempt to talk about it, they don't want to appear weak or confused so they hold back some of the truth. They try to make it less than it is, or they simply don't know how to put it into words. But even if he did, most of his friends would not be comfortable with what he was trying to say. They are uncomfortable in the presence of a man who is being emotional, showing vulnerability, needing understanding and just the right words.

How often, after a man has committed suicide, do you hear the wife or best friend say, "I had no idea," or "I knew something was going on but I didn't realize it was that bad." Tragically, the more a man hurts, and the more scared or confused he is, the less likely he is to talk to anyone, not even his wife.

Even if he does talks to someone, they don't know how to deal with a man who seems to be breaking apart. They can't acknowledge that he isn't the strong, solid rock everyone wants and needs him to be. His wife can't deal with it, and his best friend is too uncomfortable. So he continues in isolation and silence. He is alone and worries that he might be going crazy.

If he had been warned that someday this time would come, this questioning, these doubts, maybe he wouldn't have such a difficult time. But there is no set of criterion, no science to help him understand and accept that this is a normal transition.

Menopause has a clear understanding of what is happening in a woman's body with the changes in hormones and the slowing down of the reproductive system. There's none of that for men. So even when a man is brave enough to seek a doctor's advice, the doctors are just as confused as their patients. They don't know what it is, they don't know what causes it, and they don't know what to do about it. And if the doctor is a man, he has the same fears as his patient, and doesn't want to acknowledge it because it might happen to him.

Male midlife crisis is a mystery that looms out beyond view, in a fog. It's the great unknown, dark and damp, filled with deep holes. Because men, even scientific men, avoid the entire issue, it will be some time before it has the understanding that menopause now enjoys.

24

Chapter 4

Is He Going Crazy?

A man is taught from birth to repress his feelings and emotions. He's gotten so good at it that he doesn't think he has them. You've heard your husband or dad deny, sometimes quite angrily, that he might have shown a soft, tender, or vulnerable emotion.

But at midlife, when most of his goals are either achieved or–with a growing sense of disappointment–he knows they never will be, those buried feelings start bubbling up, like a geyser, ready to blow.

Reaching the middle years causes most everyone to take at least a little peek back at how they've done. It's that little peek, that moment to pause and wonder, that triggers the dark journey into midlife crisis.

Even if a man has been tremendously successful,

which, in most societies, usually means monetarily, he still has the same issues to battle as other men. Men are goal oriented by nature so no matter how many goals they achieve, there are always unfulfilled goals still to be met.

On top of the unmet goals is a sense of failure, fear that time is running out, and questioning that maybe even the goals that were achieved weren't worth giving up his life for. Because he has cut off his feelings, his emotions, his ability to get close to the people he cares about, he ponders these questions alone, in isolation and darkness. There begins to grow within him a feeling of angst caused from an awakening to the gaping hole caused from an emptiness that he never noticed until now.

The successful man–maybe even more than a man with the simpler life–is potentially at greater risk of a true crisis. Because he achieved so much, he feels like he ought to be happier than most. Because he was more focused on his goals than the average man, he has been even more disconnected from his feelings. Because he worked harder and identified himself more with his achievements, he is less likely to have strong bonds with family and friends. And it's the bonds with loved ones that can make the difference between a true crisis, a mildly uncomfortable time, or easy transition.

But for every man–whether he is successful or not–that pivotal time comes when he looks back at his life and his accomplishments, no matter how great or small.

What he sees, what he feels, is the void, the hole, the emptiness, the loneliness and isolation, that stems from the denial of his true feelings and emotions. When a man takes that look back at his life, he knows something large is missing, he just doesn't know what.

Once the feelings begin to rise to the surface, he can no longer hold them back. There are too many of them, and they're too compelling. But because he has no experience in dealing with emotions, they squish out in a myriad of ways. The real dilemma is that he doesn't know what they are.

He's scared because this is all new to him. And because he's a bubbling volcano of feelings he's never, ever allowed himself to feel, he is in a constant state of overwhelm.

You know how alarmed most men become when we women cry or act out emotionally. They are beside themselves with not knowing what to do. Can you imagine how much more disturbing it must be for them when their emotional state turns into a storm filled with lightening, thunder, gale force winds, and a deluge of rain capable of drowning him?

He doesn't know what these feelings are, or even that they are feelings. All he knows is that this is something entirely new to him. And whatever these feelings are, he knows he's not supposed to have them. He knows he's not supposed to be scared. Because he is so unfamiliar with his feelings, he worries that he's losing his mind. He's not crazy, but he feels like maybe he is, and he's scared to death.

The only way he has known how to deal with feelings in the past is to repress them. But at this stage of his life, because they are so strong and overflowing so rapidly, that is no long working. Because he doesn't recognize the emotions he's feeling, he certainly can't explain them; not to himself and certainly not to you. He can explain the inner workings of a combustion engine, but he has no words to explain what is going on inside himself.

So he suffers in silence. He strikes out at those closest to him, which is mainly you. he acts out in every way possible to make himself feel alive. He pretends he's happy with his new girlfriend, or his sparkling new Harley Davidson, and works feverishly to avoid the pain and fear caused by the bubbling inferno that is churning inside of him.

On the surface it appears that maybe he *is* going crazy, but if you can accept that he is in a great state of emotional upheaval–a true crisis of the soul–maybe you can be enough of a support that he can hang on long enough to make it through.

Chapter 5

What's Love Got To Do With It?

One feeling your husband (or boyfriend) has been allowed, and even encouraged to have, is love. Because he is daring to question his life, the validity of his goals, and the way he has organized and lived his life, he finds that isn't working either.

Men have the same need to feel and express their emotions as women. The problem is that most emotions are considered weak and feminine. That sissy thing again. But there is one 'soft and tender' emotion that he has been given the go-ahead to feel, and that's love. But the more masculine he considers himself to be, or he has been raised to be, the less *softly, the less romantically,* he will express his love. The less he can express love, the more he will suffer when he arrives at his time to 'pause' and look at his life.

He has been taught to equate love with sex. Sex is macho and manly, sex is being 'the man.' Tenderness, romance, all that 'mushy stuff' is uncomfortable for most men. When you want just to cuddle and touch, he doesn't understand because he thinks all touching must lead to sex and all sex, must lead to orgasm. "Yes! I'm the man." "Mission accomplished!" "Job well done." He can do what he's 'supposed' to do, and at the same time he never has to acknowledge his tender side.

But all human beings have a need to touch and be touched. Maybe you've read about the 'tests' they did on monkeys. When they were not touched and held, they did not develop, they did not grow, and eventually, they died. The same tests were done on human babies, and the results were the same. Lack of emotional, social, and motor development, lack of growth, and sadly, after it was too late to reverse the damage, some of the babies died.

So, even though he needs touching as much as you do, he has never been able to be vulnerable enough to admit it. Has he ever come to you and said, "I need a hug." Probably not, that's what *you* do. Since he and his buddies started discussing sex, or should I say, joking about sex, touching, tenderness, and romance were not part of the conversation. It was sex, titties, pussy, intercourse, and coming. Period.

As an adult, sex has been the only way he's known how to express intimate love, and the only way he has been allowed to fulfill his need to touch and be touched. It's the closest thing to intimacy that he's been able to experience. But at this stage he knows something is missing. It's not fulfilling his needs any longer. And he doesn't understand why.

He's been taught to accomplish goals; to see a job through to completion; to get from point A to point B in the shortest amount of time, and the most efficient method possible; to complete what he's started. For him, sex means climax. He has never seen the point of being physical with a woman without a climax. He doesn't see the point of 'making love' without at least one of them climaxing. But the feelings of deep dissatisfaction are there, he just doesn't recognize them.

Not realizing that what he wants is more emotional closeness, he assumes that the reason sex doesn't satisfy him any longer is because he isn't attracted to you. He thinks he's not satisfied with you any longer when what's really going on is he isn't satisfied with sex any longer. But what man can admit that? That would be going way too far. So he starts to look around at other women. Maybe that will do the trick. But even if he does have an affair or two, those are even less fulfilling. At least with you he has a bond of history, and knowing each other inside and out.

So no matter what he does, more sex is not what he needs. He's at a stage in his life that he wants more emotional closeness, more emotional connection, but doesn't know how to get it or even that that is what's missing.

Set a goal...achieve it. Set a goal...achieve it. It always worked, or at least he felt like it worked. And in his work, it has carried him through. He thought it was doing the same in his personal life and never understood what you meant when you said you wanted more intimacy, more touching, more time together, more talking and sharing.

But you know that isn't how it works with human interaction. You know how good it feels to share. You know that the deeper you share with someone, the more connected you feel. And you know the importance of touching.

To him, physical intimacy of any kind is only step one of the completion of the goal: climax. You've always known that cuddling, stroking, and holding each other are pleasurable behaviors in their own right, and that they certainly don't have to lead to sex and ultimately, climax. You've always known that the two of you could be closer, but over the years, when you've asked for more intimacy, he thought you meant more sex.

Sex is his way to express love and create intimacy. He doesn't realize that sex doesn't equal love, and a climax won't create intimacy. Think about how little boys, high school boys, college boys, and even young men are taught to think about sex. With all that attitude of joking, scoring, don't talk about the details, don't get too mushy, you haven't had a chance to get more than he could give.

If he feels too deeply, if his emotions are too strong, that makes him very uncomfortable. It makes him feel vulnerable. Ironically, letting himself become comfortable with feeling vulnerable is exactly what he needs. But, like all other strong emotions, even love, all he knows is to repress them and deny them as best as he can.

Most of his life, his wife or girlfriends have begged for more intimacy. It's confused him because he thinks that's what he's been doing. To him, more intimacy just means more climaxes. This method has never worked very well for you and at midlife, it's not working for him any longer either.

But he doesn't know what to do because he doesn't understand that his feelings of dissatisfaction aren't about you, they're about his inability to feel. So, too often, he assumes that he doesn't love his wife any longer and starts to pursue his need for love elsewhere. But more partners, more sex, and more climaxes will not give him what he seeks.

Chapter 6

Why Can't He Ignore His

Emotions Any Longer?

He's had feelings and emotions all along, but successfully represses them. He doesn't understand why isn't that method of dealing with feelings working any longer.

What's different about what he's feeling now is the added layer of doubt that has been creeping in. As he gets closer to midlife, his level of accomplishment, his successes and failures are clearer, more obvious. He can't help but notice. And when he notices he takes that life-altering pause to look back on his life. Usually, because there has been no real intimacy with the people he cares about, in his estimation, it feels like nothing is working any longer.

It's only a feeling deep within him, and even though he's unaware of it, can't acknowledge it, it is overpowering him...and he's scared.

He doesn't realize that what is meaningful is not the achievements or the failures, but the closeness with the people he cares about; in particular, true intimacy with you. Of course, he would never be able to articulate that.

He wants to blame it on his lack of accomplishments, which, for him, have a direct correlation to his stature as a man. But even if he had achieved every goal, he would still be experiencing the same emptiness. That's why that moment when he pauses and dares to look at his life, is such a pivotal point for him.

He has two directions he can go, either consider himself a failure or understand that he's entering a new phase of his life. This second option is not available to him if he's never been taught that what he's feeling is natural and normal.

Unfortunately, because change is uncomfortable, he chooses what is familiar. He judges his life in a linear fashion, A connects to B, which connects to C. That's how he's always done it, and it has worked. Or it seemed to have worked...up until now. But the crisis that he's in silently signals that it hasn't worked, at least not with what really matters. Dealing with people and feelings and emotions isn't a matter of checking off the steps to a goal.

When he was building his life toward the accomplishment of goals, it worked fairly well. But now that he has seen where he stands, he begins to feel the emptiness. For him, emptiness is just something to be filled up. Another goal. Harder work, a new car, a motorcycle, women, drugs or alcohol. Anything to fill the hole. But that kind of emptiness, emptiness that comes from not feeling and the distance that he has always kept from the people he cares about, is caused from isolation.

Chapter 7

Why Has He Isolated Himself?

He doesn't know he was isolating himself. All he knew was that he was doing what he was supposed to do: Work and take care of his responsibilities. He was never taught that intimacy and love were equally important to a full and rich life. Because he's never acknowledged or allowed himself to feel the full depth of his ability to love, he has kept himself in that tight fitting box. And because it's such a tight fit, there has been no room for anyone else and certainly not for all those emotions. So he sits in his box looking out at you, and you can't get near.

Midlife crisis is traumatic because the only way he is going to get through it is to step out of that box. If he does that, he will be able to reconnect the parts and pieces he discarded when he began to force himself to fit into the mold that society demanded of him.

To become a whole person who feels and expresses feelings and emotions, he must know what parts to reconnect. But he has been isolated from his feelings for so long that he can't identify them. So he grasps at whatever he can and usually it is something outside of himself.

In his effort to fill the emptiness with cars, women, drugs, working harder, he moves further from the people he cares about. Unknowingly, he is also moving further from the real problem that he must resolve, if he is to come out the other end a happy man.

Chapter 8

Does He Have To Change?

To move into this next phase of his life, he must become a different person than he has been. What worked in the past–denying his feelings and emotions–is exactly what is causing him such turmoil.

To become fully human, so he can fill the emptiness and rid himself of the isolation, he must climb out of the box he's been living in. That's scary because that means he must go to a place that is not only unfamiliar, he's been warned not to go there. He is frightened to go into this abyss of human feelings because, at some subliminal level, he fears he might fall in and never return.

In a way–if he does it well–he *won't* return. At

least not as the person he has come to know, the person who is familiar to him. But that person is the one who is in trouble. If he will trust enough to feel the full range of his emotions he will finally be able to feel whole, real and authentic. The emptiness will be filled when he can express his emotions–to himself as well as to you and the people he cares about.

Chapter 9

Who's In Control?

One of the many levels of his crisis is that he doesn't want to lose control. That's why he has suppressed his feelings. It's also why he is fighting so hard not to feel the emotions that are trying so desperately to come out.

The irony is that he's going through this crisis because he hasn't *ever* been in control. Society, family, church, teachers, coaches, and peers have been in control. They have caused him to keep his true range of feelings buried. If he can allow himself to feel all the things that are rising to the surface, he will finally be the one in control.

As he has held back his feelings from himself and the important people in his life, he has held back the possibility of living a fuller, happier, richer life. He has never learned to allow things to happen, to accept, to loosen up.

He needs to let go of old beliefs, behaviors, and all the unwritten rules that society has laid on him. That puts him in a terribly uncomfortable position because what has always made him comfortable has been the control. He thinks he's in charge, and he's unwilling to let go. But if he doesn't step out of that box, he will never be in control and he will never be able to connect to his real self or the people he wants to love.

Chapter 10

How Serious Is It?

We make fun of the male midlife crisis because the things men do to resolve it are perceived as silly, stupid, hurtful, and even dangerous. With greater levels of isolation, overwhelming feelings, divorce, and sometimes his life in shambles, suicide is the only way some men can deal with what is happening to them. The mental and emotional pain is so great for these men that the only way they can see a way out is to kill themselves.

Women attempt suicide more often than men, but they don't always want to kill themselves. They are often reaching out to the people around them. They drop hints, leave messages, and emote outwardly. They use pills, poison, or slit their wrists, which caught in time, can often be reversed.

When a man is in such severe emotional crisis that suicide becomes a viable option, it is often too late to help him. And his method will be something very permanent. Guns, hanging, crashing a car, or jumping off of tall buildings. These are not reversible.

It is telling that as men age the rate of suicide rises. Men have no outlets for expressing what they feel, so everything that has led him to the brink of suicide is exacerbated. When a man has no outlet for the expression of his fears and pain, suicide comes as a welcome relief.

Chapter 11

Do All Men Go Through It?

Because our culture teaches men to believe they must fit into the box–without ever telling him about the box–and because it begins the day he is born, all men must go through this phase of questioning. But not all will experience it as a crisis. A man who has never learned to look inward, or to understand himself somewhat, or to express what he is feeling, will usually suffer the greater level of crisis.

He's always been isolated but because his focus was on the achievements still in front of him, he never noticed. When a man's full energy is spent on the achievement of goals, of succeeding, he is too busy, too preoccupied with the future. As he gets to that time in his life that he can't help but look at what he has accomplished, he begins to feel the angst of the big question that lurks at the forefront of the male midlife crisis: Is this all there is?

Every man must come to terms with this question. Some do it better than others. Better in that they cause themselves less harm, and better because they learn to become fuller human beings who have put the missing parts back in place. Once they learn how to feel and express what they're feeling, they enjoy a richer more fulfilling life.

Most important is for him to not be afraid of the questions, and the feelings those questions bring to the surface. If every man had been exposed to what you're learning here, men would fare much better, and they would live richer lives. If that were the case, that pivotal question wouldn't even come up.

Chapter 12

Why Are Men So Unprepared?

Men do not discuss what's going on inside of them, especially not with other men. So they assume they are the only ones going through it. The isolation is self-induced. It would be good if men would talk about it with each other. But because they aren't in touch with what's going on until they've gone through it–if even then–they won't admit to themselves, or anyone else, what they are feeling.

Another big part of their crisis is that they can't admit to being weak, unsure, or vulnerable. It's part of the unwritten pact between men. At a certain level, they never let go of that little boy in the playground who would be devastated to be called a sissy. The adage, "Never show your cards," is part of the, "never do anything that could cause you to be called a sissy...ever."

It would be much better if men could understand that embracing all of their feelings. If they could accept them as a sign that they're more fully developed as a person, rather than seeing them as a weakness, the subject of midlife crisis would be mute.

Chapter 13

Is Anyone To Blame?

You are the source of his intimacy; you are the source of love, and you are the one he looks to in order to create the warmth and safety within the relationship. But you are not to blame for what he is going through. Yes, he blames you because you are the one he expects to give him what his soul is seeking. But you can't give it to him because you don't have it. Society took it away from him, and he is so unfamiliar with it that he doesn't know what he needs from you.

Ironically, it is what you've wanted all along. When he was first in love with you, his feelings were so strong that he couldn't help but express some of what he was feeling. That same man is the one you've hoped would rejoin you in your relationship. The good news is that if he makes it through without causing too much damage, it's likely you'll have that man you fell in love with so long ago.

He is the one who threw the feeling part of him out of the box, by believing what others told him to do, by believing what it means to 'be a man.' But he shouldn't blame himself. Society–and especially his peers–were just too strong a force. He didn't know he was dissecting himself, and if he had, he wouldn't have known where to store those feelings for a future day.

It's no one's fault, but he is the one who must go on an inner quest in search of his true self. He's lived only a portion of who he can be, he is the one who feels lost, he is the one who has isolated himself. He is the one who has to put the pieces back together.

Some Native Americans have a ritual where the boy goes out into the wild to find his manhood. It is the primal right of passage. He must go through fear, hunger, anxiety, and deep soul-searching in order to return to the tribe as one of the hunters, as a man, no longer a boy.

In a sense, the modern man must go on a similar quest. But this is the reverse of what that Native American boy was doing. He must go and find the feeling boy who he lost touch with so long ago. He must go through fear, hunger, anxiety, and the same deep soul searching to connect to all the lost parts of who he truly is. If he has done his job well, he will return from the 'wilderness' a new man.

If he is blaming you, it is only because he is afraid to go out into the wilderness alone. He wants you to make it all better, like you always have. You have been his haven, his only real source of love. You have been his guide in the relationship, the one who has used your compassion, your softness, your tenderness to resolve any problems you have had together. But this is beyond you. This is a job for him alone. No one can look inside for him. He must do that himself.

It is important that you not blame yourself. It has nothing to do with you. You have not failed him. If anything, you have seen that there was more to him and tried your best to assist him in allowing it to show itself. But he was too afraid to be that vulnerable. Being alone was easier, safer, and more familiar.

Now that he has no choice but to feel what is bubbling to the surface, he strikes out at whoever is closest, and that happens to be you. At this time it is best that you leave him alone, don't try to explain to him what is happening, and don't try to get him to explain it to you. He can't, and he resents being put in a position of weakness.

Women are quick to feel guilty for everything that isn't going right, even when they had nothing to do with it. You have been trained to take care of others, to anticipate their needs, to keep them emotionally safe. Because you have been responsible for making the relationship run smoothly, you blame yourself when it doesn't work as it should.

In the past, you might have made changes within yourself and in your behavior so your relationship worked. You were able to keep the peace. But now, because he is in such an emotional upheaval, you can't do anything that will help him.

Chapter 14

Why Can't You Help?

"We've got to toughen him up," the father says to the mother. She wants to protect her son from being hurt but if he runs to his mother, his friends jeer, "What's the matter? Mamma's little boy?"

There's that time in every little boys life when he must leave his mother's side and join the rough-and-tumble world of males. You try to gather him up into your arms, and he says, "M-o-o-o-m!" and looks around to be sure no one sees.

So he can't cry, he can't ask for help, he can't touch, and he can't express fear, sadness, or pain. But what about the "good" feelings? That's not allowed either. If he's joyous, or blatantly in love, or feeling silly, even that gets teased out of him. And there's no way he's going to show tenderness, except in the rarest of moments.

Now is the time that you can help him, but he's too conditioned not to ask for help. We all joke about a man's inability to ask for directions, that he would rather drive around lost–not admitting it, of course–than stop and ask someone where he is.

This is the same kind of thing. He can't ask for help in his crisis because that would admit he is not capable of 'handling the situation.' He can't go to you because you, of all people, are the one he feels most obligated to show his strength. Remember? He's your rock. And he does not want to disappoint you. Something he has never told you is how important it is for you to respect him. Everything he is feeling right now makes him need to hide it even more.

If he's like most men, he won't go to the doctor until he's half dead. And you know how he will respond if you say anything about following the doctor's orders. Then there's the whole therapist thing. More than any time in his life, he could use a good therapist but it's beyond fathoming. No way will he allow himself to be that vulnerable.

Any comments or advice you offer causes strife. "What's going on with you? You just aren't here. You're somewhere else," you lament. And his usual response is, "Get off my back. I'm just preoccupied with a lot of things on my mind." "But there's obviously something wrong. You're distant, grumpy, and you've been ignoring us. Can't you tell me what's wrong?" But he doesn't want to deal with you, so he snarls, "Just leave me alone," and walks away. There's nothing you can do and you feel helpless. You blame yourself because you feel like there's something you should, or should not, be doing.

58

Chapter 15

What Can You Do?

He's probably not going to come to you for advice or to
share what he's going through. More likely, he's been
lashing out at you, or ignoring you, isolating himself
further. And you've learned it's not okay to try to get
through to him. You can't get him to tell you what is
going on, and you can't point out that you suspect he's
going through a midlife crisis.

If you can't help him, and he won't come to you,
what should you do? You won't want to hear this, but
your focus needs to be on taking care of yourself, and
your children if you have them still living at home.

You're going to have to step back and let him do
whatever he's going to do, because he's going to do it
anyway. Be loving and supportive from a distance.

Stop trying to get him to explain what's going on, and avoid confrontation.

It's a bit like taming a wild horse. He'll buck and kick and run in circles, but eventually, he'll wear himself out. But in his 'wild' state of mind, he might do and say things that are very hurtful. Just steer clear and don't go into the pen with him. That would only exacerbate the issues that are being acted out.

As hard as it will be, do not take any of it personally. He may say things that surprise you, blaming you for everything that has ever gone wrong, and whatever he perceives is the state of his life.

Do not respond. Simply imagine his words floating over you, unable to hit their mark. Yes, it's okay to feel hurt, angry, and resentful, but do so when you are alone. Don't engage him because it could end up pushing him over the edge of the precipice that he's been standing on.

It is important that you step away from what you're feeling and be smart. Because so many men ruin their family's finances at this time, make sure you take care of you and your children. If there is a savings account, move some into your own account. If you fear you will not be able to make ends meet, get a job right away.

He may leave and move in with another woman. Just remember that it's not about you. It's not the same as when men have affairs. This is about his emotional survival.

Because he's unlikely to look inward, he'll still be hurting. He's using the new woman, or the new car, or trip around the world as a way to avoid the feelings that scare him. Do your best to let him be that wild horse, knowing that he will eventually tire himself out. He might or might not want to repair the damage he's doing, but that should not be your primary concern.

Focus on taking care of yourself–both physically and emotionally. Do some serious soul searching of your own. Look at where your marriage could be better in case he makes it through and realizes he wants to be with you.

Spend time with your women friends, but try not to talk about what's going on so your soul can get a reprieve. Give yourself some space to breathe, to laugh, and simply be. And respect his privacy. Don't say anything you wouldn't say in front of him, except with a close, trusted friend who will respect what he's going through.

Spend time in nature so you can reboot, cleanse, and recharge your energy. Enjoy the sunshine, breath fresh air, especially if it is near moving water so you can benefit from the negative ions. Go barefoot on the earth because it will help you balance your energy from within.

Take that class you've been putting off for…how long? Go to lectures, read books, get involved in a charity organization. What does you heart want, outside of your marriage? What have you denies yourself, or neglected? What did you stop doing so you could focus on your marriage and raising children? Do those things now because it will help keep you occupied, but more important, it will help you become a better version of yourself.

If you are interested, I offer online workshops that are designed to help you discover who you really are, what you want, and what you can do to let go of whatever has held you back from living the life you were meant to live.

Do your best to come to terms with the fact that your marriage might not survive the devastation. My advice in this chapter is not about you saving your marriage. It's about saving you. He is going to do whatever he must, whether he's consciously aware of what he's doing or not. There is nothing you can do to change that, except stay out of his way and not engage him in arguments.

If you remind yourself that he has to go through this if there's any possibility of rebuilding your lives, you will be better equipped to deal with the turmoil.

Another way to look at it is to think of what he's doing as a tornado that's forming over there in the distance. You see it coming your way, so you gather all your supplies and go down into the storm cellar. There, you can hear the storm above, with winds blowing, buildings breaking apart, and debris flying everywhere. But you're smart enough to know that it would be crazy to go up there to see what's going on.

So you stay in the cellar, safe, with what you need to make it through the storm. Eventually, it subsides and once you feel sure it's over, then you go up and check.

What you see is devastation all around you. But you also know that with work, it can be cleaned up, and you can rebuild your life.

There is no certainty about how this will end, but I can tell you from personal experience, that if your marriage does not survive, you will. And because you took charge of your life, and didn't allow his crisis to rip you apart as he's done to his life, you will be a better, smarter, stronger woman. And you will be much better equipped to build an even better life for yourself.

My husband's midlife crisis turned out to be a great gift to me, because I was able to take what I was learning about myself and grow beyond my wildest expectations. Yes, it was horrible as I was going through it. But even then, I had trust that no matter what, I would come out of it a better person. And I did. I have thanked him, and he knows I am sincere because he knows how much I benefitted, and how my life has transformed into the magical thing that it is today.

That can happen for you when you take the opportunity being handed to you to discover who you truly are. You will benefit if you use the lessons as opportunities to blossom into your most amazing self.

Chapter 16

Where Will It End Up

Male midlife crisis is a very private matter, at least for what the man going through it is feeling. There are no statistics on it, and certainly no way of rating the severity of what each man is going through.

There is no way to predict how a man will deal with that pivotal question, "Is this all there is?" Maybe your husband, or sons will be open to reading this. That could make all the difference. If you do pass it along, don't ask them if they read it, or what they thought of it. Just hope that they're interested enough to want to see what I have to say on the topic. Let it be their private way of learning about a topic that is ignored by most men, sometimes feared, and most often, laughed about.

There is also no way of predicting whether or not your marriage will survive. If you do decide to try and rebuild your marriage, here's what I suggest.

Imagine that you are starting fresh, with a new marriage. Because in a way, you are. If he wants to come back and make it work, he is a new man. Like the young Native American, he has gone on a quest and come out a man. He'll be more in touch with his feelings, and he will have discovered that it's not the goals he was taught to pursue, but family, love, and intimacy that make life worthwhile. He will have become the man you've hoped he would be.

If you look at this new marriage as a design project, like building a new home, you can have it be exactly the way you both want it to be. Talk about what you hope, what you want this new marriage to include, how you will handle the various 'jobs' that are part of keeping a home functioning properly. Decide who will do what, but not simply because that's the way it's always been done. See this as a design of something entirely new, with each aspect of your marriage talked about, and decisions made together.

And be prepared to renegotiate–or redesign–what has not been working the way you want. Focus on taking care of each other, of being more loving, respectful, and kind than you've ever been. Make a pact to recommit to each other and your marriage at regular intervals. Make this a project that you work on together.

If you like this idea, you can get my book, *Save Your Marriage and Fall In Love Again* on Kindle, at Amazon.com. It is a step-by-step guide to building the marriage of your dreams.

If you can save your marriage, you can have a better life than you ever imagined. But that will only happen if you take this time to work on yourself. Get to know who you really are, what your heart desires outside of your marriage, and what makes you feel fully alive. Pursue those interests, learn about yourself, discover parts of you that you never knew where there and honor and celebrate them.

You are a magical being, full of life and potential. Allow those dormant parts of you to blossom and shine. Be the woman you've always wanted to be, and invite more of you to emerge than you imagined was possible.

If you stay true to yourself, and trust that no matter what, your life can be amazing, it will be. I am living proof that it is possible. If you feel a connection to me, It will be an honor if you join my Inner Circle at KaraOh.com. There I offer every tool imaginable for you to discover your True Essence and encourage it to flower in all its beauty.

I hope this book has been helpful and that you are not as scared as you were before you began reading. I hope you feel empowered with new understanding of what he is going through, and why. If you can see what has been expected of him simply because he was born a male, your heart will open. Then true compassion will allow you to bless his journey for what it is, and hope he comes out a happy man.

It's possible. But most important, take care of yourself. Don't get caught in his storm. Be supportive, but do not ignore what you need to be safe and to take care of your physical, emotional and spiritual needs. Because you are a woman you are strong, able to bend in the wind, and continue to grow, no matter what.

I wish you blessings on your most fascinating journey, the journey toward the very best person you can be. For it is in that that true happiness lies.

Kara Oh

Printed in Great Britain
by Amazon